Poetry for Men

A Book of Romantic Self-Expression

By The Poet of the Great River

Rock Cottone

RiverRock, Inc., Publishing Division
St. Charles and St. Louis, Missouri

Poetry for Men
By Rock Cottone

Published by RiverRock, Inc.
St. Charles and St. Louis, Missouri
P.O. Box 210205
St. Louis, Missouri (MO) 63121
Phone: (314) 610-9999

First Printing, 2000

Printed in the United States of America.

Library of Congress Catalogue Card Number:
00 091701

ISBN: 0-9700728-1-3

This book is dedicated to

Torre Alexander Cottone

All royalties will be donated to the Muscular Dystrophy Association and the Duchenne Parent Project for Muscular Dystrophy Research.

Table of Contents

Part I

SELECTED POEMS

(SOME OF THE AUTHOR'S FAVORITES)

HIGH ROMANCE
(February 20, 1994)

Close moves,
Stroked curves,
Profile of an angel,
Nerves calmed,
Fear asunder,
Soft touch,
Romantic thunder.

Scented lightly,
Fashioned slightly,
Moving slowly,
Loving tightly.

Grasping, gasping,
Driving, firm,
Grappling, tumbling,
Passion's turn.

Embracing in a rhythmic dance,
The magic of a high romance.

Loving fools in soft embrace,
A unity,
Transcendent grace.

FOR I AM THE POET OF THE GREAT RIVER

(This poem continues on the next page)

I know now who I am.
I am the poet of the great river.
For I am the river,
And the river is me.

Living near and living in
The depth and torrent,
The gentle bent of trees along the shoreline,
The rocky chain that bridges what is otherwise unbridged.

Dispersed,
Yet never averse
    to insult,
    intrusion,
    or diffusion.

Limited, but unlimited,
For nature's way will test artificial boundaries at their best.

Powerful, yet gentle to the touch.
Colorful, yet blended as the sunlight glistens with the wind,
Along the surface one can enter in
    to change its course –
Submerge and feel the force.

Filled with life,
But lifeless.
Filled, but accepting no matter what the cost.
Filled or empty, nothing has been lost.

Poisoned from the outside;
Filtered by relentless contact with an underlying riverbed--
    sometimes hard,
    sometimes soft,
    sometimes shifting by way of pebbles and the sand,
    sometimes gentle to the hand.

Venturing forth or regressed,
It never stops at giving to the rest.
Connected, but unending in the end,
It's free to travel,
And to others it may send
A message about living at its best.

Yes I am the poet of the great river.

ANGEL'S SONG TO FATHER*
(February 17, 2000)

Place your cheek by mine
And look up to the stars that shine,
For you are the father of an angel child.

Take comfort here.
Relinquish all you fear.
The promise of a healthy child I cannot give.

But know that I have been restyled
To rise up to the brightest star
Against the darkest night.

And as my body fails,
My wings will sprout
To take me on a journey
To a place where spirits soar,
And earthly limits are no more.

I feel your warmth nearby.
Rejoice in knowing I will fly
Unfettered by a corporal cast,
As time relieves me of its grasp.

And though you may feel little solace,
It's important that you know this:
An eyelash wisp, an angel feather,
We are one, now and forever.

(*This poem was originally titled "Angel's Song to Mother" with a subtitle of "Torre's Song.")

"DON'T GO AWAY"

Howdy Dooya?
Kangarooya.
Hop along, a sing along song
  bird flying in the sky
  king and queen for just one day.
Beaver – leave it to your way.
A life of Riley honeymoon
  early news too mighty
                Minney
  mouse cartoons.
A net, a few nets,
  cello singing in a clan,
Road running coyote,
Super, man.

MOLLY'S PRESENCE
(1994)

I laid me down to sleep—
  to rest me—
To let me heal torn tired sinew,
To let my body feel anew.

I closed my eyes and felt your breath upon my lashes,
Caressed by love,
A press of flesh upon my forehead,
With hair a muss,
But lightly brushed
By fingers by my temple …

Your love has made life simple.

For in this moment of your absence,
I sensed and felt love's awesome presence,
And knew that we were one.

THE TREE BY THE ROAD
(1971)

With gusts of power that stifled my senses,
The wind blew wild over fields, through defenses,
And I knew that the blizzard was greater by far,
Than I, on a back road, alone in my car.

I struggled and fought with the car's steering wheel
Cursing others I blamed for the dreadful ordeal,
And I plowed through the snow thinking only of time,
Seeing life as if death was its only design.

Still the car moved quickly with the time just as fast,
Nothing mattered to me, not even the past,
For all was disdained as the pavement I traced,
Not even the snow cooled my time-maddened pace.

Then I glanced to the left at a frozen dead tree,
And cold-piercing branches pointed straight back to me,
And I looked at the tree, and it burned in my eyes,
As I saw lives of men, and I heard children's cries.

And I felt the disgust of a person insane,
And I faced all disease and was seized by the pain,
And I held in my arms a dead babe of a war,
Then I saw what was me, cold and looking afar.

So I moved my mind quickly as to regain compose,
But the thought of the tree lingered still in repose,
For I was afire by the message unsaid
By the tree by the road that looked icy and dead.

I lifted the gas, but no motion was slowed—
I was sitting, I was nowhere, with nowhere to go …
I was sitting, I was nowhere, with nowhere to go.

FREE SPIRIT
(1974)

Live free spirit,
Live in the wind,
  in the sun,
  in all life.
Exist in me in everything I do,
Exist, for me.

Carry forth my happiness!
Spread far the joy I love,
And I will kiss the splendid flower
  to let my tear moisten it soil,
As I bend low in humble praise
  to the beauty I adore.

Never ending … life never ending.
Lust's urgency is more than sex, in love.
In love, free spirit, exist in me –
Create for me.

Dispel all myth of death in me.
Dispel all fear of hate in me.
Engulf me in your arms, so warm,
                                        so soft,
And lose me in your breast.
At last, you lead the way.

BE CAREFUL
(1993)

Dominant male
Chasing tail.

Be careful
Or you'll catch a glimpse
Of something that will make you wince
In pain one always sees the light
That keeps one waking through the night.

Are lust and love one in the same?
Am I her lover or a game?

Be careful.

MY FATHER'S EYES

(May 17, 2000)

(This poem continues on the next page)

Massive arms,
A barrel chest,
A mighty handsome man,
Taut, tan, strong.

By childhood eyes,
At work,
Side-by-side,
The scent of his sweat
Seared by the sun,
With dust and dirt
Against his white t-shirt,
Boundless grit
Determined to get the job done.

By childhood eyes
Grown wise by years.

Father,
Mentor,
Teacher,
Friend,
The hand that steadied
My maiden voyage on a two-wheeled Schwin,
And corrected every awkward lean
Along the road of life.

Now stymied
By nature's twist,
Tremulous,
Weakened by the burden
Of the unrelenting march of life,
Withered,
Wrinkled,
Shrunken,
With eyes still wise,
My father's eyes,
He now still leads the way,
As my hand steadies
Every step along the path.

ARUAL SNIKREP: THE BACKWARD NAME IS JUST THE SAME TO ME

A little animal came into my life,
And made me think,
And made me sigh,
And made me laugh,
And made me cry,
And made me strong,
To make me weak,
To show me love,
To show how neat insanity can be.

A feat it is to feel a surge,
A sudden urge to kiss the forehead
Of the monkey
In the woman
Who you are.

And I am just an ape.

And just the same,
As clear as things have come to be,
I'll stand upon my head,
And laugh,
And sigh,
And scratch my elbow with my eye,
And kiss the earth to tell it, "Hi!"
And never ask, not once, just why?

REARISING AFTER RAISING
(October 17, 1997)

Just a glance
Inspires lustful feelings.
Attraction is not lost ...
Just set aside.
Raising kids -- prioritized.

Special moments rearising,
Special feelings,
Fleeting, but deep-felt.
Someday these flashes will not go unanswered,
As responsibility is set aside
To reengage what was once engaged,
To replenish the soul.

Part II

A FATHER'S POETRY TO HIS CHILDREN

IN AWE OF CHRISTOPHER

They handed you to me,
The son I'd longed to see,
A babe in arms so strong
            but weak not knowing how to cradle love so fresh,
                        so fragile to caress one's soul
                                    in depth of feeling whole.
Your skin was moist and soft,
Your cry turned tender with the light touch of the flesh,
And I was filled with pride and joy
            just gazing at my little boy.

TO MY SEVEN-YEAR-OLD KRISTINA
(1993)

I was tired when
I put my head upon your lap.
You put one hand upon my head—
  the other stroked my stubbly beard
  then pinched my nose,
  then doubled back to rub my chin –
You giggled as I broke a grin.

Your fingers were so little
  'gainst the backdrop of my massive head,
But they were filled with magic
  and a type of love inbred.

I gazed up at your face in awe
  as we shared this moment together,
Nothing could replace the draw
  of two souls as one forever.

IN BABYLAND HEAVEN

(A poem to Maria, December 5, 1995)

Blue-eyed baby doll,
Makes us want to hold you while
You cry a little tearless cry …
Just crying 'cause we don't know why.

We'll put you to your mother's breast
To let you get a little rest
In babyland heaven.

Cooing, gurgling,
Lifeline suckling.
Surviving is the best you can,
Assisted by a father's hand
And mother's love.

Some day you'll stand
Beside us as an image of our love,
A gift from heaven up above…
Babyland heaven.

TO TORRE ALEXANDER
(April 7, 1997)

My little son
You are the one,
By a name
We are the same.

Father,
Brother,
Now another
Male child,
Love-styled
By a mother,
Coddled to her breast,
Time to get a little rest.

I put you on my chest
To feel your strength,
Full climbing length,
A belly like a mountain top,
Hop after hop,
You reach your goal.

I know you'll reach another goal,
As life will challenge,
You will manage
With knowledge of a father's love …
Poetic adulated love.

ON STANDING NOT ALONE
(To Cristiana, June 1, 1999)

The first time that you stood your ground,
You held your head up, made a frown,
Then realized you'd reached the heights,
As angel wings held you upright.

A smile came quick across your face,
As toddlerhood with new found grace,
You broke a kind of silly grin,
Then raised your eyebrows, then your chin,
Enough to throw your balance down
To let your bottom hit the ground.

Bewildered, but with new found grit,
Not content to wait and sit,
You must have stood up forty times,
The night of babyhood's demise.

Your dad and brother watched in wonder
As baby girl found toddler splendor.

KIDLET DAD

They grab me,
Pull me,
Wanna nab me.

Horsey ride,
Legs like a slide,
"Come on big man –
count ten and hide."

Tossing, squeezing,
Tickling, pleasing.
Chasing, seizing,
Playful teasing.

Poke an armpit,
Make 'em squeal –
Then release them,
Make 'em feel
The joy of conquest of a man
They think a giant who's gone mad …
Then they giggle, "Kiss me dad!"

Part III

POETRY TO MOLLY

RELINQUISHED
(December, 1993)

I saw you from across the room.
I knew then our lives were forever intertwined.
Don't ask me how I knew.
The intuition was deep felt,
overpowering—
long lasting—
disarming.

My heart surrendered at that moment,
gave over to you –
relinquished.

Can we come to grasp the meaning
of two souls meant for one another?

The search is over.

All relationships past and present – child's play –
For one cannot deny when sparks fly.
One cannot deny the chemistry of love,
As hope and passion interplay,
Dreams unknown fulfill,
As love embodied we instill.

Innocence,
Sensuality,
Lust.
We break the rules because we must.

I hold you in my arms and feel strong,
Press my chest against your flesh and feel whole,
Kiss your lips to open eyes as they penetrate my soul.

I give over to you—
Relinquish.

OF FEMININE DESIGN
(January 19, 1994)

A masterpiece,
Exquisite,
And reflecting of deep colors,
From a mold most certain broken
By the gods as gesture token.

Don't ornament perfection,
Give rise to full perception
   of this beauty to adore.

Like nothing else encountered,
A woman-child
   so softly styled
   as carved within a stone
          by chisel strike,
          by chisel strike,
A masterpiece of feminite
Without the had of man alight.

A mold?
A stone?
A chisel strike without the hand of man?
A masterpiece most certain from the heavens, understand
This masterpiece embodies all the good of womankind –
The passionate,
The sensuous,
The feminine design.

"BE ROOSTER"
(January 26, 1994)

Cock a doodle do,
I love to peck with you.

A rooster strut,
Suck in my gut,
This old cock's got a little chick,
A prairie hen, a little hick.

The other males
Are chasing tails,
But I'm content –
One chicken's scent.

The chick's around,
Kick up some ground,
Stick out my chest,
She wants to nest.

Some peckin' here,
She's nipped my ear,
The mating cluck,
And I'm so stuck.

Cock a doodle do,
I love to be with you.

PUERTO VALLARTA
(June 1, 1994)

Pounding
Sounding from the waves,
Salted air with misty haze.

Seagulls passing in the wind,
Concentric circles closing in,
Lifted by the breath of seas,
Wings held firmly to the breeze.

Days of loving by the sea,
Feeling sensual, strong, and free.

MISS MOLLY JEWEL
(January 24, 1994)

My purpose is clear,
My destiny defined,
Immortalize Miss Molly,
My lady jewel enshrine.

Illumination,
Demonstration,
In words poetic captivation,
Put down in words this fascination.

No pedestal's too high,
For words can't truly capture
My love, my lust, my rapture –
Her beauty to adore.
She's feminine, so sensual,
Earth's little jewel has leashed this fool,
Forever at her beck and call,
The pedestal will never fall.

Put pen to pad,
Put words to rest,
Refine, restyle at her behest,
This poem must be perfect
As the subject is a gem,
Formed deep within the earth,
With open heart one must descend
To touch the spirit in this woman
Only man can understand,
To touch the jewel of the feminine …
A man with pen in hand.

A TOUCH OF SILK
(May 5, 1994)

I felt your silk within my hands
And pressed it gently to my face.

A fragrance rose up gently,
And the taste of you aroused me,
As my senses were entranced
By your vision scent enhanced.

Your love's a godly gift
Which I treasure more each moment,
As my life moves to fruition,
And each day's a new addition
To a story to be told,
Of a love that's never ending,
As new feelings do enfold.

I celebrate these flashes,
Embracing perpetuity,
While living you as long as we can share one breath,
Love sentient with passion's scent
'Til time unleashes life from me,
A touch – a flash – eternity.

WEDDED ADORATION
(March 18, 1995)

My lady love
Sent from above
Do take my hand,
As we do stand in mutuality,
To pledge eternity.

Love embodied in an act of passion,
Hosted, growing,
To be fashioned in an image
  that is shared of those who came before,
An image for posterity,
An image of our progeny.

And we do hold in gentle hand
A promise by an act of faith –
To have,
To hold,
To activate our spiritual prosperity,
In love,
In trust,
Romance has grown prophetic of love's verity,
Made known through wedded adoration.

Part IV

POEMS TO LOST LOVES

AS SPIRITS BLENDED IN THE WIND

(This poem continues on the next page)

You gave me a poem today
That touched the very soul of me.
So real were the images that flowed from your pen
That I felt you were there –
        that moment in time,
        that image of mind,
        those feelings in rhyme.

Our love is timeless
In an unsure future,
Where prediction is lost
        in the present …
        in the past.
How long can we last
When the chains bind so fast?

Can love transcend time spent together?
Can we embrace a memory
        as we embraced as lovers—
        an immaculate unity
        denied an eternity—
        obsessed?

Is it coincidence or happenstance?
Can this happen out of chance?
Or is it a test by a power greater than ourself?

I want to hold you
But don't know how.
As friends?
As lovers?
As spirits blended in the wind?
As childhood sweethearts born again?

When emotions are under reign
I can separate the pain
And fake a microscopic look
At something greater than myself.
But when emotions tide
All pretense and defense
Go by the wayside,
As I sense our presence
Penetrating inside,
And as I visualize your eyes,
Face to face in soft embrace,
I know I love you,
I will always love you.

ON SEEING YOUR EX-LOVER AT THE LAKE

I felt you for a moment there,
Among your friends your past did tear
A hole along your heart and soul.

It hurt me just a bit
To see emotions fit
A pattern that is all too clear,
To touch one's soul, to bring one near
Such feelings and the reign of tears.

I wanted just to hold you then,
But did not really know you when
This fateful moment came to pass.

The fact that we were just new friends
When lovers could have made amends
Did not seem fair,
As we did share this moment in the sun.

I promise you,
We will be one.

BE STILL

Be still and let the pain remain,
For the love of one who's gone,
For the love of one, restrain.

Feel it deep
To feel it seep
Into every crevice of the soul.

Anguish, anger, fear, desire,
Burning, searing, passion's fire,
Know it as it ought to be.
Know a love that should not be—
Everlasting.

AND TO MY LOVE
(1970's)

Just as the sun permeates the darkness,
I'll touch you,
And daylight will fill the once dark skies,
And someday we'll have child.

THE ENDLESS OTHER DAY

That night I pulled her to my chest.
I kissed her forehead
And caressed her gently to the heartbeats that were one.
In love, together we did stay.
In love, together, in our way,
We touched the endless other day.

THE SPIRIT OF A DOVE

I miss her.
I miss her smile,
Her laugh, her cry, her gentle style.

Why must a love so true
End in a flash of blue?
What rules of men were made to steal
A love so true to make one feel
Alive, so young, at one with self?

Be selfless and do sacrifice
What one can't give – a future life--
entrusting love –
Do sacrifice.

The pain I feel – it goes both ways.
Her pain is mine and mine the same.
She gave me love; I felt it, too.
She gave herself, and I was true—
So true to know the spirit
In a woman free to soar.
So true to know my love for her
Would bind her evermore.

Procreant urge is more than sex in love,
Yet intuition does protect
The spirit of a dove.

SURRENDER

Touch me
Oh one who changed my life,
For beauty of youth,
Innocence and truth.

Spontaneous bi-seduction,
Lust's fateful attraction,
Once lost – but not again.

I need to hold you,
To press your skin,
Be hypnotized within.
So let it be
That souls are one again.

Drop the defense,
As nature's drive
Will settle all the rest.

Full blooded senses,
As what is meant
Will be embodied hence.

Surrender.

MEMORIES
(Early 1970's)

High school honey
Took my money,
Now I'm broke
And all I have is memories—
Damn expensive memories –
Priceless.

CAPTIVE
(1970's)

All snow is rain,
It's all the same,
'Less you are there to catch a flake upon your
tongue,
And I am there to watch.

ALICIA

Alicia, a lady,
Alicia, a rose,
Alicia you came to me
As fate's deep secret told.

Magnificent – your beauty,
Magnificence behold,
As fingertips touch lightly,
To tighten, clasp, and hold.

Eye to eye as spirits fly,
Mind in mine will never die,
A unity unequaled,
As feelings do enfold.

So deeply felt emotions,
So true to touch one's soul,
In love, in lust,
Enveloping,
Surrendering, yet bold.

My innocence – be gone!
Your innocence retold,
As teenage zest rekindles
And adult souls remold.

Alicia, my lady,
Alicia, my rose,
My love for you – unending,
My time with you – pure gold.

DUMPSTER LOVE

Hiding, hiding,
No confiding,
This is not love's "suppose to be."
This will hide what others see.

Dumpster, bumpster,
(I'm the bumpster),
Better there than by a tree,
'Cause that's where others can see.

Embarrass,
Humping,
Always bumping,
Moon's too bright to hide the sight,
Cover up full moon tonight.

Forbidden, hidden,
Lovin's rubbin',
I wish to love more openly,
To celebrate your love for me.

PART V

ON MANHOOD, SENSITIVITY, SELF-AWARENESS, AND GROWTH

SEVEN A.M.

(Early 1970's)

(This poem continues on the next page)

Where am I?
Geez, it's cold here –
Alarm is clanking in my ear.
I'll reach it, touched it,
        damn thing, missed it – got it.

These sheets are warm,
The bed so soft,
Another minute I'll be off somewhere a sawin' logs.
If I can keep one eyelid open –
There I did it – got it open –
Feels so heavy,
Softly spoken words are coming to my mind …
A girl,
A voice,
Another time …

Ahhh, almost did it,
But I didn't.
I'm awake,
Yes, I'm awake,
I'll make it.

Funny how it felt so good.
My feet so warm…
Head kept on sinking,
What did it harm to stay on thinking
One more minute softly sinking?
One more minute thinking that it's rainy out –
Pitter patter rainy out.
I bet it's damp and hazy out –

The haze over the fields,
A blanket for the wheat
(A blanket for my feet),
A cloud so white and soft,
(Can't keep my head aloft),

Softly on the brink of heaven
Heaven sinking into heaven,
Softly sinking in my mind …
A girl,
A voice,
Another time …
About eleven.

CONTACT

Sometimes I feel so down on life,
And then,
I gaze up and see myself,
And there I am.

SUN WORSHIPPER

Listen.
While sunbeams beat a rhythm
Down upon the ocean waves,
A man rests quiet, silent,
As the warmth reflects
Upon his naked self.

ON CREATIVITY

Can stand the pain,
Can stand the pain,
As what emerges from the womb –
The ultimate creativity.

THE POET

A poet carries forth an unborn child.
She waits.
It grows.
And then in one creative burst,
She touches what is formed.
A poem, then, is born.

He fathers it,
He strengthens it,
He stands up in defense of it,
Then sends it on its way.

THE DYING SCENE

There's beauty in a dying man,
The beauty left by nature's hand as time goes by …
And what we see
Of dying eyes so filled by dream,
Can make death seem
A living part of living's end,
And a beginning unknown by men.

AS ALWAYS

(This poem continues on the next page)

Rocco roomie,
Buddies' buddy,
Coping hoping,
Always funny,
Always sunny
Never tries his bony nose upon the rocky road.

Open doors and doughnut swirls,
Cup of coffee,
Twinkie softly squeezing chewsy,
                                        chewsy,
                                        pewsy –
Spit the lousy twinkie twinkie.

Lousy Suzy wants some sex,
Farm-house lewsy,
Hay in hair and hair like hay.

Cap and gown –
A crown of thorns with funny horns
As on the bull made mad by men.

Lover on the wake of morn –
Wash your armpits.

Cast a pearl in soft ice cream,
Swirling like a twist of toes.

Resting pesting,
Always nesting birds in trees,
And buzzing bees.

Gee whiz kid,
SPAZZO,
Pass the brass and stand the sass.

Laughs and cries,
And tears of flies,
And upside-down cake world –
Wonder wonder world –
As always.

HARD BOILED
(Early 1970's)

Ouch,
Ewww,
Eeee,
I touched a girl who sprung a leak—
She left her love at home to keep.

I grabbed,
I nabbed,
But on she blabbed,
She slobbered on my face.

Yet confident, I kept on trying,
                                        lying,
                                        prying …
I couldn't stop the harmones flying.

Still, on she talked
As on a ride through fairyland …
A never-ending ride.

Oh, what a mind she had to match
What hatches from an egg,
And I, a fool to try to make
A chick whose love is hard to take.

IN MEMORY OF GRANDFATHER (ROCCO)

There was a man,
He lived according to his right,
And lived life fully 'til one night
When time released him from its grasp.

He was a man,
Much criticized,
Who lived a code made noble by a dream.
And when he lived, he stood above all else.
Alas, he died with nothing but that dream.

There was a man,
He did not know that I would stand,
His life imprinted deep into my soul.
And I will live a man who knows the wisdom that he gave,
And he will live within me,
Until my dying day.

DEEP DOWN

Something's in there,
Way down in there,
Inextricably trickably
covered by the mire—
Inexplicably mimickably
moaning as I grow'n.

SWEET WINE

Sweet wine is born from fruit
conceived by seeds
imbedded in the dirt.
Some say that we are born the same.
How unpalatable.

THE PRECIOUS ROSE

How beautiful the rose—
The rose is a precious flower,
A flower like no other,
Within a bush of thorns.

How beautiful the man who moves gently,
Who tenderly reaches forth and plucks the rose from where it grows,
Who carries forth the memory of its defense,
And caresses every petal, hence, just as the first.

How beautiful this man—
The rose is his,
And that is all that any man needs.

SUCCESS
(Early 1970's)

One hand,
My hand,
A defenseless hand,
Always reaches,
Always with care,
Hoping to touch something beautiful.

THE FEMALE PARADOX

Women seek dominant males,
And then they spend their lives
Trying to dominate them.

LOVE
(Early 1970's)

For the love of the one,
The one nearest my dreams,
I would give all my love – all my life.

And I'd give not to hold,
But to touch …
And she'd give just that much back to me.

AT THE LOUNGE

A dollar here,
A dollar there,
That builds the flirting egos high
Among the men who show their strength
And women, who move as if meant to give
  their bodies at the drop of coins,
Do twinkle as they roll toward the dancehall floor.

WHAT HAPPENS TO LOVE?

What happens to love?
A lustful past,
Impassioned,
Just the presence of the other
Excites the senses.
Harmones flow,
Powerful feelings,
Driven.

And time does pass,
And life does pass.
Does familiarity breed contempt?
Must familiarity lead
Attempts to reengage lost emotion?
Is biochemistry corrupted,
Unrectified
By tides of passion
Slowly decreasing
By a failing gravity
Like satellites spiraling out of orbit?

And what is left,
When friendship fails,
And each encounter
Pounds a nail into the coffin of love?

How sad.
How moribund.

What is the answer to stem indifference?

MEDITATION
(Early 1970's)

Spin the mind,
A dreamer's dream –
The seamstress weaves
Unceasingly,
Within the cobwebs of a space unknown.

Look up,
Look down,
And all is lost
To gain momentum to be tossed
  within the bounds, uncircumscribed
    by any semblance of a thought.

Confusion of the senses:
Turn toward defenses,
Truncate and obfuscate their core.

Mind masturbate without a word,
Throw retrospection out the door,
And all is lost, yet all is gained,
And lying still is still the same –
Unstill as it may seem.

No breath, no sound,
Yet all is clear that is around—
Around around it goes.
And where it stops is upside-down
By right-side-up perspective.
By right, by left,
By right inherent in a soul
Left undefined to unbehold.

AND HE SMILED

(This poem continues on the next page.)

Age eighty was this man
Who they said did daily run
'Cross the barren desert ground
Colored by the setting sun.

And I laughed, I thought it odd,
But the townsmen thought me sad,
For they saw this man a god,
And I – a naïve lad.

They smiled sarcastically
Saying "Go and see this man!"
So that evening I did hide
Near the path by which he ran.

Long I waited in the heat,
As my sweat began to stream,
Then I saw him from afar,
And I thought my sight a dream.

Yes he ran toward the sun
With the rays upon his face,
And it seemed to make him strong,
As he ran with rhythmic grace.

And the god called "Mercury"
Would be jealous at the sight
Of the man with winged feet
O'er the hot engulfing blight.

Oh, I gazed amusedly,
From the scene I was inspired,
As I felt his countenance,
Which I knew I did desire.

Is it true the gods do live?
Sweet delusion rectify --
For what's strong is weak in turn,
And what lives in turn must die.

Thus my ecstasy did fade,
As I saw something was wrong,
For his pace became too slow,
And his face became too drawn.

Then he grimaced as in pain,
As he gasped and grabbed his chest,
And his legs became so weak
That they failed him – then the rest.

Downed spread-eagled in the sand
With his head turned to one side,
He reached up toward the sun,
And he smiled just as he died.

GRADE SCHOOL
(Early 1970's)

Hold out my hand?
Don't slap—
That hurts you ugly bitch,
I bet you are a wicked witch.
The window's close,
And daydreams here are all I know …
And you would take what I do love away?

Go teach to someone under rule,
I'll live my life a dreamin' fool,
And make it just the same.

THE RIVER

Cry as it travels to unknown goals,
Flowing as I travel with it.

Slowly moving,
Ever present,
Without disguise
Omnipotence or ties.
Bending, yet unbending.
Touching all that touches all.
Changing, yet unchanged.

Moving gently downward to its end,
The remnants of its journey it will lend
To something greater than itself.

Upon my knees I gaze,
I touch it.
In humble praise I lie down in it
Upon the shallow floor.
And there I'll be,
Forevermore.

ABOUT THE AUTHOR

Robert Rocco ("Rock") Cottone was born in St. Louis, Missouri on January 28th, 1952. He was raised in the post World War II Italian-American culture in the suburbs of St. Louis and had a story-book boyhood right from the pages of Mark Twain. He would ride his bike for hours to watch the barges at the Alton lock and dam, and was enthralled with the power of the mighty Mississippi. He attended Catholic grade school (Our Lady of Good Counsel) and later switched to public schools in the St. Louis suburbs, graduating from Hazelwood High School in 1970. Although he lived a rough and tumble boyhood, playing war games in the wooded areas near his home, he was always considered a sensitive child by those who knew him best. During the Viet Nam War he remained stateside and was a medic in the Air Force. He later attended the University of Missouri-Columbia and earned a degree in psychology. Much of his early poetry was written during a period of personal reassessment during his undergraduate days. He continued his studies earning an advanced degree in counseling at the University of Missouri-Columbia. He earned a Ph.D. degree at St. Louis University in 1980. He is currently a licensed psychologist and a Professor of Counseling and Family Therapy at the University of Missouri-St. Louis. He has authored over 60 professional and scientific articles and two books, Theories and Paradigms of Counseling and Psychotherapy (1992, Allyn & Bacon) and Ethical and Professional Issues in Counseling, with Vilia Tarvydas (1998, Prentice Hall).

In 1975 he married Laura Perkins. They had two children, Christopher Rocco and Laura Kristina. They separated in 1992. He is currently married to Molly Jo Conley, and they have three children, Maria Francesca, Torre Alexander, and Cristiana Danielle. Torre suffers from Duchenne muscular dystrophy, a fatal genetic disorder. He dedicated this book to Torre, as his love for his son has caused a major reevaluation of what is important in his life. All royalties will be donated to the Muscular Dystrophy Association and the Duchenne Parent Project for Muscular Dystrophy Research.